My Firs k

Amazing Animal Books
Children's Picture Books

By Molly Davidson

Mendon Cottage Books

JD-Biz Publishing

Read More Amazing Animal Books

Purchase at Amazon.com

Download Free Books!
http://MendonCottageBooks.com

Table of Contents

Facts about Kittens

Kittens turn into cats that can live up to 20 years.

Kittens need their mothers for six weeks before going to a new home.

Kittens eat their mother's milk, until they are old enough to eat harder cat food.

Kittens cannot see or hear when they are born.

Kittens are considered kittens until 2 years of age.

Adopt a Kitten

© Sara Robinson - Fotolia.com

There are many kittens in shelters waiting to be adopted, this is a great way for you to get a kitten, and it helps save that kitten.

Kitten Care

After kittens are off their mother's milk you will need to make sure they are fed.

Kittens should NOT drink cow's milk, they need kitten milk, and this can be found at your local pet store.

Your kitten will need to be taught where to go to the bathroom, either outside, or in a litter box in your house.

You will need to bathe your kitten. It is best to grab it by the nape (back) of its neck, this way it cannot scratch you.

Make sure to be gentle, don't get soap in his/her eyes, and help them feel safe, not scared.

© Katrina Brown - Fotolia.com

Newborn Kittens

Kittens are in their mother's stomach for 64 days before being born.

They cannot see or hear, so they find their mother by smelling her scent.

Mother cats will carry their kittens around by the nape (back) of their neck, this doesn't hurt them.

© **Cherry-Merry - Fotolia.com**

If you love, cuddle, and are kind to your kittens from the very beginning of their lives, they will grow up to be nice and friendly.

Black Kittens

© Naty Strawberry - Fotolia.com

Many people believe black cats are bad luck, but this does not include black kittens.

Black kittens need just as much love as any color kitten.

White Kittens

Most white kittens, are Persian, they are white and fluffy.

© jojobob - Fotolia.com

Persian Kittens

© beneteau13 - Fotolia.com

Persians originally came from Persia, giving them the name, Persian.

They are known for their fuzzy, long fur, and short nose.

A lot of Persians have blue eyes.

They are very sweet cats and love attention.

These are meant to be inside loved, cuddles, and spoiled.

Tabby Kittens

Tabby kittens have many colors of fur, grey, orange, black, brown, tan, in a stripped pattern.

A tabby kitten will have an "M" in their fur in between their eyes.

© **cynoclub - Fotolia.com**

The word tabby is talking about the pattern they have on their fur.

Siamese Kittens

Siamese cats come from Thailand and the breed started from the Oriental cat.

Most Siamese kittens are white, with dark ears, nose, feet, and tail.

They are very social, and need to feel lots of love.

© cynoclub - Fotolia.com

Bengal Kittens

© Krissi Lundgren - Fotolia.com

The Bengal cat looks like a leopard, its fur has markings with stripes and dots, and sometimes they have a white belly.

Bengal cats can be kind of wild, so be careful if you get one as a pet.

Kittens and Puppies

Kittens and puppies are most of the time very best friends.

They are both very childlike and playful, they love to play together.

They both discover new things with by smelling.

© Gelpi - Fotolia.com

Read More Amazing Animal Books

Purchase at Amazon.com

Website http://AmazingAnimalBooks.com

Our books are available at

1. Amazon.com
2. Barnes and Noble
3. Itunes
4. Kobo
5. Smashwords
6. Google Play Books

Download Free Books!
http://MendonCottageBooks.com

Publisher

JD-Biz Corp

P O Box 374

Mendon, Utah 84325

http://www.jd-biz.com/